reaching out to
THE BAPTISTS

with heart and mind

William J. Whalen

LIGUORI
PUBLICATIONS

One Liguori Drive
Liguori, Missouri 63057
(314) 464-2500

Imprimi Potest:
John F. Dowd, C.SS.R.
Provincial, St. Louis Province
Redemptorist Fathers

Imprimatur:
+ Edward J. O'Donnell
Vicar General, Archdiocese of St. Louis

ISBN 0-89243-209-8

Excerpts from *Vatican Council II: The Conciliar and Post Conciliar Documents,* edited by Austin Flannery, O.P., copyright 1975, used by permission of Costello Publishing Co., Northport, New York 11768.

Excerpt from *A Baptist View of Changes in Roman Catholicism* by C. B. Hastings used with permission of the Southern Baptist Home Mission Board.

Table of Contents

1. They Must Be Doing Something Right

Taken together, the two dozen Baptist denominations in the United States form the largest family in American Protestantism. About a decade ago the Southern Baptist Convention (SBC) nudged the United Methodist Church out of first place among Protestant denominations in this country. Since then the Baptist margin has widened; and, with 14 million baptized members in all 50 states, the Southern Baptists now have no close competitors. Between 1972 and 1982 the SBC grew by twenty percent; during the same decade most mainline Protestant Churches either declined or barely kept up with the normal population increase.

Baptists comprise the majority of church members in ten out of the eleven states of the Old Confederacy. They practically dominate the religious life of such states as Georgia, North Carolina, Texas, and Alabama.

Outdated stereotypes of the Southern Baptists persist. James Sullivan, a recent president of the Southern Baptist Convention, commented: "A world that had thought we were an ignorant, barefooted, one-gallused lot was jarred out of its seat when it found out that our voluntary gifts in a year are approximately

$1.5 billion, and that on an average Sunday our churches baptize about three times as many people as were baptized at Pentecost." They staff the largest and the third largest semiaries in the world; in fact, one out of every five seminarians in the United States attends a Southern Baptist institution. The SBC supports 6,600 missionaries at home and abroad. Total value of SBC property exceeds $13 billion. As the New South has taken its place in education, wealth, and power, so have the Southern Baptists.

The various Baptist branches — Southern, American (Northern), black, and smaller Baptist sects — form the largest group of Protestants in the United States. Yet, world-wide they are far outnumbered by Lutherans, Anglicans, and Presbyterians. Of the world's estimated 31 million Baptists, only 4 million live outside the United States.

In an average week the Southern Baptists will baptize about 8,000 new members. Attending its Sunday Schools are some 7 million pupils, often picked up and delivered by fleets of buses.

Baptist ranks include millions of humble Americans, black and white, whose names are unknown beyond their neighborhoods or hometowns. Yet, the Rockefellers are also Baptists, and so are many Texas oil barons and Sun Belt entrepreneurs such as the Hunt brothers. America's best-known evangelist, Billy Graham, left Presbyterianism at the age of seventeen during the fervor of a revival and sought ordination in the Southern Baptist Church. Reverend Martin Luther King, Jr., Nobel Prize winner, pastored black Baptist churches in Montgomery and Atlanta before spearheading the national civil rights movement. The erudite Bill Moyers holds credentials as an ordained Southern Baptist minister.

2. *Where They All Come From*

COMMON ROOTS FOR MANY BRANCHES

In a sense, the Baptists can be considered spiritual descendents of the Anabaptists once removed. The Anabaptists began about 1525 when a group called the Swiss Brethren rebaptized themselves and refused to align with either the Lutherans or Calvinists. The idea of Baptism by immersion as the only valid form was to come much later.

The best historical evidence places the foundation of the Baptist movement in a small congregation of English refugees who had settled in Holland. Their leader, John Smyth, was a Cambridge graduate and an Anglican minister who had adopted Puritan and Separatist views. In 1609 in Amsterdam, Smyth and his followers started a new congregation called the "Church of Baptists," which was based on believer's Baptism. His co-worker, Thomas Helwys, returned to England in 1611 and founded several Baptist groups. The Baptist movement spread throughout England, but never gained a large following there.

American Beginnings

Roger Williams, who founded the first Baptist Church in the American colonies, remained a Baptist for only four months. He left England in 1630 and settled in the Massachusetts Bay Colony. His convictions, including his belief in religious freedom, led to his banishment in 1636. He bought land from friendly Indians and founded Rhode Island. When he accepted the Baptist position on Baptism, he had himself rebaptized in 1639 and, in turn, baptized eleven followers. Later that year he resigned from his pastorate, and for the rest of his life called himself simply a "Seeker."

Despite opposition from the Congregationalists and the Anglicans and the favored status of established Churches in all but two of the colonies, the Baptists made some headway. By 1700 there were 14 Baptist Churches in America, and by the end of the century that number had grown to 1,152. Unlike the Anglicans and Methodists, many of whom supported the Crown, the Baptists wholeheartedly favored the colonists in the Revolutionary War.

While other denominations depended on an educated ministry, the zealous Baptists sent hundreds of preachers, with little more than a Bible and a hymnal, to the frontier settlements, to the South, and to the blacks. Along with the Methodist circuit riders, these Baptists won converts in the West and South which would put these denominations in the forefront of American religious life in the nineteenth and twentieth centuries.

The Baptist revival exerted its greatest appeal among the workers and small farmers. The basic theology, democratic organization, de-emphasis on ritual, and availability of enthusiastic if uneducated ministers all promoted the unusual growth of the Baptist Church.

The Seventh-day Adventists and the Disciples

Some Baptists took other paths. A Baptist preacher named William Miller calculated that the end of the world was nigh and gathered a band of believers to await the millenium. When the predicted day in 1843 came and went most Millerites fell away, but a remnant would reorganize as the Seventh-day Adventist Church. Alexander Campbell left Presbyterianism and embraced the doctrine of believer's baptism, but he later disagreed with the Baptists on other questions. His movement developed into the Disciples of Christ and the Churches of Christ; together these denominations claim almost 4 million American members.

Slavery and the Civil War

Although every major Protestant denomination, except the Episcopal Church, divided over the issues of slavery and the Civil War, most of them have since reunited. The Methodists came together in 1939 and the Presbyterians in 1983, but the split in Baptist ranks has never been mended.

Baptists in the South opposed abolition, even though they were less likely to be slaveholders than the wealthier Episcopalians and Presbyterians. When the Baptist Foreign Mission Society refused to appoint any slaveholder as a missionary, the Southern Churches seceded and formed their own Convention in 1845. A leading Baptist spokesman at the time, the Reverend Richard Furman, declared: "The right of holding slaves is clearly established in the Holy Scriptures, both by precept and example."

At the time of the North-South division in 1845, about 130,000 of the 351,000 Baptists in the South were blacks. Slaves sat in the galleries of local churches. Eventually, the freed slaves formed their own Baptist Churches and national organizations.

Blacks and the
National Baptist Convention, USA, Inc.

The oldest of the black groups, the National Baptist Convention, USA, Inc., reports 5,500,000 members. In 1915, a split within this body resulted in the formation of the National Baptist Convention of America (2,668,000 members). Another schism in 1961 drew many supporters out of the "incorporated" group to form the Progressive National Baptist Convention, Inc. (521,000). Several smaller bodies draw their memberships from the black community.

Ethnic Origins

Besides the major Baptist bodies, a score of smaller groups attract Baptists with a strong ethnic background or a dissatisfaction with the theological stance of the larger Churches.

Two Baptist groups were formed to minister to converts from German and Swedish backgrounds. One is the North American Baptist General Conference, with 43,000 members of German ancestry; the other is the Baptist General Conference, which was originally entirely Swedish. Today the BGC counts 133,000 members, but only about half of its pastors are Swedish Americans. This small Conference sends 140 missionaries overseas.

Other Baptist Churches serve members of French, Hungarian, Danish, Italian, Finnish, Norwegian, Polish, Romanian, Mexican, and Czech ancestry. Some are bilingual; others conduct all services in a foreign language.

Differences of Outlook

A few groups of Baptists go back to the seventeenth and eighteenth centuries. The Seventh Day Baptists observe Saturday rather than Sunday as the day of rest and worship. Their first congregation was established in Newport, Rhode Island, in 1672; they now number only 5,200.

With the slogan "Free grace, free will, and free salvation," the Free Will Baptists are strongly anti-Calvinist. They started in North Carolina around 1727. The issue of slavery split the Free Will Baptists, and in 1910 those above the Mason-Dixon Line merged with the northern Baptists. Those in the South continued their separate existence and now number 228,000. Blacks organized the United Free Will Baptist Church.

The United Baptists represent the continuation of an eighteenth-century movement in North Carolina and Virginia. Most of the 63,000 United Baptists live in these two states and in South Carolina and Kentucky.

The 72,000 Primitive Baptists oppose Sunday schools, mission societies, denominational organizations, and youth groups.

They date their history to the early nineteenth century. Also known as "Hard Shell," "Anti-mission," and "Old School," they are strongly Calvinist in their theology. They claim to be completely faithful to the New Testament; so much so that if the Bible has no record of mission societies in apostolic times there should be no such innovations in the twentieth century. Their ministers need no college or seminary training, and their churches usually serve the people of backwoods areas of the South. The National Primitive Baptist convention is the black counterpart and claims a membership of 250,000.

The 24,000 General Baptists, who formed their organization in 1870, represent the Arminian rather than the Calvinist theological orientation. Their 900 churches in the South and Midwest admit all professed Christians to the Communion table. Unlike the strict Calvinists, they admit the possibility that a born-again Christian can fall from grace.

Fundamentalism

Finally, in this century, there is a group of Baptist Churches which have been founded, usually, in a protest over the alleged liberalism of the parent body.

Fundamentalists tried to gain control of the Northern Baptist convention for many years. They organized in 1920 as the Fundamentalist Fellowship. Despairing of winning the majority of their fellow Baptists to their stand, they broke away in 1947 to form the Conservative Baptist Association of America (225,000 members). Another schism in northern ranks in 1932 had led to the formation of the General Association of Regular Baptists; their 243,000 members manage to support 1,644 home and foreign missionaries.

Members of the American Baptist Association, who are also known as "Landmarkers," believe that the only true Christian Churches are Baptist Churches. They refuse to accept the label "Protestant" since they maintain that the Baptist movement antedated the Protestant Reformation. This denomination began when a group broke away from the SBC in 1899; the present name was adopted in 1924. In most matters they closely resemble the Southern Baptists, but they tolerate less organization. They number 1,500,000.

In 1950 the American Baptist Association itself suffered a schism which led to the organization of the Baptist Missionary Association of America. This group is militantly fundamentalist, and its 224,000 members emphasize missionary work.

Also part of the Baptist family are such tiny groups as the Two-Seed-in-the-Spirit Predestinarian Baptists, the Duck River (and Kindred) Association of Baptists, and the National Baptist Evangelical Life and Soul Saving Assembly of the U.S.A. The General Six Principle Baptists report only 175 members in 7 congregations.

3. *Where They're Going*

KEEPING THE FAITH OR SPREADING IT

Until the end of World War II, the Southern Baptists concentrated on building their strength in the Deep South. Here they dominated the religious life of many communities or sometimes shared this role with the Methodists. Some Southern Baptist churches occupied entire city blocks which included the church, Sunday School, parsonage, youth center, etc.

A Historic Decision

The Southern Baptists made a historic decision in 1950. They decided to abrogate the gentlemen's agreement with their estranged northern brethren and invade the North and West. Since then the Southern Baptists have gone into all fifty states and have become a national denomination in fact if not in name. If the Northern Baptists wanted to start congregations in Tulsa or Richmond, they were welcome to do so; meanwhile, the Southern Baptists planted outposts in New York City, Milwaukee, and Minneapolis. In 1942 there were only 41 Southern Baptist churches in California, but 40 years later this had grown to more than 1,000 with 350,000 members.

The apparent malaise which has overtaken the Northern Baptists was one unadvertised reason for the Southern invasion. Devout Baptists below the Mason-Dixon Line believed that the liberalism and coldness of the Northern Baptists were turning off potential converts. Furthermore, the migration of many people from the Bible Belt to northern cities and suburbs called for establishing Church homes which would be familiar and supportive.

By 1983 the Southern Baptists had founded more than 36,000 local churches. Most of these Baptist churches enroll fewer than 300 members, but some are huge. Eight SBC congregations report more than 10,000 members.

By far the largest SBC congregation is the First Baptist Church of Dallas, which enrolls 22,000 members, employs a staff of 125, and occupies 5 city blocks. The church seats 2,500 worshipers, and the Sunday School provides instruction for 8,000 young people and adults. Popular radio commentator Paul Harvey belongs to this church as did the billionaire oilman H. L. Hunt. The annual budget exceeds $7 million.

Southern Evangelism and Education

Most of the major Protestant denominations have cut back on missionary activity, but the Southern Baptists now support more than 3,200 men and women in the foreign missions and 3,430 in home missions. They labor in some 100 countries. In the United States their missionaries make special appeals to Hispanics, Jews, and ethnic groups.

Most Baptist-related colleges and universities are rather small liberal arts colleges with 1,000 to 2,000 students. By far the largest Southern Baptist institution is Baylor, with an enrollment of 10,000, followed by Furman, Richmond, and Wake Forest.

For more than a century the Lutherans supported the largest network of Protestant parochial schools in the country. Recently, they were overtaken by the Baptists who now enroll 232,000 pupils in their own elementary and secondary schools, compared with 218,000 in Lutheran schools. Dissatisfied with the secularism, lax discipline, and the outlawing of prayer in the public schools, Baptists have established hundreds of parochial schools during the past two decades.

Enrollment at the six Southern Baptist seminaries stands at an all-time high. Southwestern Baptist Theological Seminary in Fort Worth, with 3,470 students, has become the largest seminary in the world.

A Threat to Southern Fellowship

The growth of the charismatic movement among Southern Baptist churches poses a new problem for a denomination which stresses the autonomy of each congregation. An estimated 100 Southern Baptist churches, with at least 10,000 members, fall into the charismatic or neo-Pentecostal category. They encourage speaking in tongues, healing, interpretation, prophecy, etc. Dr. W. A. Criswell, pastor of the First Baptist Church in Dallas, has called speaking in tongues "senseless, insane, and idiotic" and labeled the charismatic movement an "aberration and heresy." In 1976 churches in Texas, Ohio, and Louisiana were disfellowshipped by local Southern Baptist associations for their charismatic activities, but this action did not sever their ties with the SBC. How a Church which upholds the complete independence of each local church can discipline any church or church member is a vexing problem for Southern Baptists.

The Northern Baptists

In contrast to the fast-growing SBC, the American (Northern) Baptist Churches in the U.S.A. have not kept up with normal population growth. Their 1,600,000 members are outnumbered by the 2 million Southern Baptists in Texas alone. The American Baptists (Northern) have been more liberal, ecumenical, and socially involved than their southern brothers.

Northern Baptists founded such institutions as the University of Chicago, Carleton, Colby, Denison, and Kalamazoo. American Baptists support about 300 missionaries in Burma, India, Bengal, Thailand, Japan, Okinawa, and the Philippines.

Ministers and laity switch allegiance from Northern to Southern branches of the Baptist family with a minimum of inconvenience, but differences remain in such things as open Communion, ecumenism, and theology. Reunion seems doubtful.

The Black Baptists

Booker T. Washington once remarked that if you met a black man who was not a Baptist or Methodist, someone had been tampering with his religion. The great majority of churchgoing American blacks belong to predominantly black Baptist and Methodist denominations; the black Baptists alone enroll some 10 million. Traditionally, the black Church has served as a community center as well as a spiritual home, and the black minister has assumed an important leadership role among his people. Reverend Jesse Jackson is a contemporary example.

In beliefs and Church government the white and black Baptists share similar positions. Fraternal relations have been cultivated among the various Baptist groups, but no move toward a merger of the Churches is evident.

Southern Baptist Convention officials estimate more than 300,000 blacks now belong to SBC congregations; many of these belong to integrated congregations, but most attend the 750 predominantly black SBC churches.

The Independents

Perhaps the best-known Baptist preacher in the nation besides Billy Graham is the Reverend Jerry Falwell, founder and head of the Moral Majority and pastor of the Thomas Road Baptist Church in Lynchburg, Virginia. His church does not belong to the SBC but represents a growing number of congregations which are independent of any larger Baptist affiliation. Many of these independent Baptist churches make effective use of radio and TV, operate fleets of buses for Sunday School, build huge church buildings, and grow through the ministry of charismatic and flamboyant preachers.

4. What They're Like

STAUNCHLY INDEPENDENT COMMUNITIES OF THE "SAVED"

Baptists usually consider the Protestant Reformation a job half done. Luther and Calvin left too many Catholic traditions undisturbed and tolerated too many "unbiblical" practices such as infant baptism.

The Anabaptist condemnation of infant baptism found no support from Martin Luther or from John Calvin, founder of the Presbyterian and Reformed tradition, who stated: "Let us present to God our infants to whom he has assigned a place among the members of the church."

The real Reformation, according to the Baptists, took place in America with the rise of their movement which jettisoned all creeds, formal ritual, the sacramental character of Baptism and the Lord's Supper, infant baptism, and recognition of any authority beyond the local church. One Baptist slogan has been: "No human founder; no human authority; no human creed."

Sophisticated Baptists no longer identify the original Church of their denomination as the First Baptist Church of Jerusalem.

Some do believe that the early Christians were fundamentally Baptist and that today's Baptist Churches are the only ones in harmony with New Testament Christianity. In their view, later accommodations to secular authority, contamination by Greek philosophy, and the rise of bishops and the papacy introduced errors into the Christian community.

For all Baptists the Bible is the "authoritative rule of faith and practice," but not all Baptists by any means adopt a fundamentalist approach to the Scriptures. Unlike most Christians, the Baptists pay no attention to hierarchies or apostolic succession or creeds.

Being "Born Again"

When Jimmy Carter called himself a "born-again" Christian, many of his fellow Americans were puzzled. The label comes naturally to millions of Baptists and other evangelicals. Basically, being born again means that the individual has experienced a personal encounter with Jesus Christ which has transformed his life (John 3:1-15). To most such Christians the experience can be dated and timed.

Despite their name, the Baptists do not consider Baptism essential to salvation. What is essential is the individual's profession of faith in Jesus Christ which must precede water baptism. In other words, the individual must be "born again" before asking for baptism and membership in the Church.

"Adult" Baptism

Baptists and their Reformation-age predecessors insisted they were only carrying the Protestant principle of justification by faith alone to its logical conclusion when they condemned infant baptism. If the believer must confess his faith before baptism, an infant obviously could not qualify. They rejected the proxy role of the parents and godparents, and taught that only those old enough to make a profession of faith in Jesus Christ should receive Baptism. Some of those baptized by Southern Baptist congregations are quite young; in one recent year these churches baptized 1,812 preschoolers, 35,725 children between the ages of 6 and 8, and 99,085 between 9 and 11. In effect, Baptists reject "infant" baptism but do not limit the ordinance to "adults" in the usual understanding of the word. They do expect the candidate for Baptism to have reached the age of accountability and to articulate a profession of faith.

Baptism by Immersion

Baptists have always been concerned about the proper mode and age for Baptism. They believe that the only scriptural method is complete immersion; pouring or sprinkling water will not do. They reject the sacramental view of Baptism held by most other Christians and consider the ordinance of Baptism to be symbolic. As such they explain that immersion better symbolizes the death, burial, and resurrection or rebirth of the believer in Christ.

Of course, other denominations also insist on immersion: the Disciples of Christ and Churches of Christ, Mormons, Seventh-day Adventists, Mennonites, and Jehovah's Witnesses. The Church of the Brethren prescribes not one but three complete immersions as the proper Christian initiation.

Roman Catholicism recognizes the validity of Baptism by immersion as well as by pouring. In fact, until the thirteenth century immersion was the common form of Christian Baptism. It remains the usual form of Baptism in the Eastern rites of the Catholic Church as well as in Eastern Orthodoxy.

The new General Introduction to Christian Initiation in the Roman Catholic Church states: "Either the rite of immersion, which is more suitable as a symbol of participation in the death and resurrection of Christ, or the rite of infusion may lawfully be used in the celebration of baptism." Few Catholic churches have been equipped to accommodate the baptism by immersion of adults, but new church buildings will probably be designed to provide this "more suitable" mode of baptism.

Not only the form of baptism and the age of the baptized come under scrutiny by Southern Baptists; many congregations also doubt the validity of any baptism by immersion not administered by a Baptist minister. Converts from denominations which also practice immersion may sometimes be asked to undergo a second baptism. On the other hand, many American (Northern) Baptist churches admit transfers from other denominations into fellowship even though they were baptized by pouring or sprinkling as babies.

Baptismal Rite

The baptismal pool is usually situated behind the pulpit but screened from view during regular worship. Baptism is never a private or family affair but a rite administered before the assembled congregation. The pastor and the baptismal candidates, robed in white, stand in the pool. The minister proclaims: "In obedience to the command of our Lord and Savior Jesus Christ, and upon your free and public acceptance of him as your Savior and Lord, I baptize you, N______, in the name of the Father and the Son and the Holy Spirit. Amen." Some Churches perform baptisms in rivers and ponds.

The "Saved"

While Roman Catholics and most Protestants work out their salvation in fear and trembling, the Baptists affirm "once saved, always saved." The Southern Baptist Convention expressed this belief in more theological form in its 1963 statement of faith:

All true believers endure to the end. Those whom God has accepted in Christ, and sanctified in His Spirit, will never fall away from the state of grace, but shall persevere to the end. Believers may fall into sin through neglect and temptation, whereby they grieve the Spirit, impair their graces and comforts, bring reproach on the cause of Christ, and temporal judgments on themselves, yet they shall be kept by the power of God through faith unto salvation.

Worship and the Decision for Christ

Baptist worship is generally informal and nonliturgical compared with Catholic, Episcopalian, Lutheran, and other

Churches. The Sunday service always includes hymns, Scripture readings, spontaneous prayers, and sermon. Almost every Sunday service includes an "invitation" or "altar call." At this time nonmembers are invited to make a decision for Christ, and members may take the opportunity to rededicate themselves. The minister usually wears a business suit during worship, and the church itself is unadorned. Other than Sundays, the only "holy days" observed in Baptist Churches are Christmas and Easter. Local congregations may hold special services for Thanksgiving, Memorial Day, or Mother's Day.

A church may schedule the Lord's Supper once a quarter or once a month. Most Southern Baptists limit participation in Communion to baptized Southern Baptists, while Northern Baptists welcome all Christians. Baptists hold a memorial supper view of the Communion service, although a few of their theologians have begun to emphasize the sacramental nature of the Eucharist. The average Baptist in the pew rejects the sacramental understanding of the Eucharist held by most Christians — Roman Catholic, Eastern Orthodox, Lutheran, and Anglican.

In the words of the statement of the Baptist Faith and Message adopted by the SBC in 1963: "The Lord's Supper is a symbolic act of obedience whereby members of the church, through partaking of the bread and the fruit of the vine, memorialize the death of the Redeemer and anticipate His second coming." Influenced by the temperance movement, Baptists substituted grape juice for wine in the Lord's Supper.

Independence of Local Congregations

Another hallmark of Baptist belief has been the complete independence of the local congregation. The larger Convention may suggest programs and standards of belief, but ultimately the authority lies within the autonomous local churches. Each Baptist congregation adopts its own constitution and bylaws, church covenant, and confession of faith. It can choose to participate in an association (perhaps the churches within one county), a state association, and a national body such as the SBC.

Some Houston pastors once demanded that President Truman be expelled from the Southern Baptist Church because he admitted he enjoyed a glass of whiskey now and then. Truman snorted, "These Baptists can go to hell," and reminded them that only his local congregation could expel him. His home church was unlikely to ask a President of the United States to leave its ranks, and Truman was quite correct in denying any other Baptist body any authority in the matter.

A Baptist congregation can decide whom it wishes to ordain a minister and whom to call as pastor, establish the order of worship, elect its own deacons, shape the direction of its Sunday School programs, decide who is qualified for Baptism and who is to be disfellowshipped. It can set its own educational standards for the minister; many of the larger congregations expect college and seminary training, but others welcome a clergyman who has only a high school diploma.

Ministry Standards

Baptist congregations shy away from setting any educational requirements for ordination to the ministry; this allows some rural and black churches to ordain high school dropouts if they wish. Once a congregation has chosen a candidate for ordination, it invites neighboring pastors and deacons to participate by examining the candidate's theological knowledge and spiritual fervor. A church which temporarily lacks a minister can even call on lay people to preside at the Lord's Supper.

The ultraconservative Baptist Faith and Message Fellowship tries to ferret out seminary professors (who would be considered conservative by most other denominations) who lean toward liberalism or doubt the verbal inerrancy of the Bible. Scholars employing methods of Scripture criticism common in Catholic and Protestant seminaries often face difficulties in Southern Baptist institutions.

The Tension of Freedom

The fierce independence of each of its 36,000 local churches and the effort of the Southern Baptist Convention to maintain orthodoxy lead to some tension. Several controversies may exacerbate this tension. Is there any way the SBC can discipline a local church which encourages speaking in tongues and faith healing? What about Baptist congregations which go ahead and ordain women as ministers despite the stand against the practice by the SBC? Already 200 women have been ordained as ministers by Southern Baptist Churches, but none pastors a church; no one knows how many women have been ordained as deaconesses. Can the SBC take action against a pastor or seminary whose liberal theological stands go beyond Baptist toleration?

Ecumenism

Southern Baptists view most ecumenical efforts with suspicion and skepticism. They fear any infringement on the autonomy of the local church and anything that smacks of "super church." Yet, they have engaged in several fruitful dialogues with Roman Catholics as well as with the Eastern Orthodox, Jews, and Buddhists. SBC theologians have developed cordial relationships with representatives of the Glenmary Missionary Fathers.

A president of the SBC in the mid-1960s expressed a view probably held by many Southern Baptists in the 1980s: "We do not accept the ecumenical premise that denominationalism is the scandal of Christianity, wasteful, selfish, or sinful. The variety of churches produced by the Protestant Reformation has brought great vitality and strength to Christianity. Division has multiplied the Christian witness. Struggle, tension, and doctrinal debate have purified truth and have been beneficial rather than harmful. To abolish denominationalism would be to reverse the Reformation and turn the clock back to medieval Catholicism."

Social and Political Concerns

Baptists have always plumped for strict separation of Church and State. The major Christian denominations have been or are now Established Churches in certain countries: Roman Catholic, Anglican, Lutheran, Eastern Orthodox, and Reformed. The Baptists have not been.

Baptists bristle at any violations of Church and State separation, but their neighbors sometimes wonder at their selectivity. If groups of Southern Baptists agitate for a ban on beer or bingo or the teaching of evolution in the public schools, they are convinced that they are working for community betterment. Their non-Baptist neighbors may see this political action as an imposition of particular religious views on the larger community. Federal aid to Baptist-related colleges and hospitals also tests Baptist dedication to complete separation.

The ban or limitation on use of liquor has been a Baptist concern for many decades. "The production, sale, distribution and consumption of alcoholic beverages is the greatest of all social problems in the estimation of Southern Baptists" (*Social Ethics Among Southern Baptists, 1917-69*). Total abstinence and a return to national prohibition remain SBC positions.

Popular sermon topics in SBC churches include the evils of drinking, gambling, pornography, divorce, homosexuality, tobacco, lawlessness, sexual permissiveness, and sometimes even dancing and card playing. They have never considered the various types of birth control to be anything but a medical question. Ministers stress the stability of the family and the permanence of marriage but seldom raise a problem if a divorced member seeks to remarry.

In 1979, a statement of Social Principles by the SBC Christian Life Commission explained that "total abstinence from gambling, smoking, and alcohol and other harmful drugs is a preferable position for a Christian in our culture today." The statement also said: "In regard to abortion, euthanasia, and organ transplants, the decision at times is in the gray area when the choice may be between the lesser-of-two evils. Baptists generally believe, for example, that an abortion is justified only under very serious conditions: when there is a clear threat to the health or life of the mother or possibly in the case of a pregnancy as a result of incest or rape or manifest deformity of the fetus — cases that are extremely rare."

5. Getting Acquainted

GROWTH AND MOBILITY ARE BRINGING US TOGETHER

Almost all Baptists live in the United States, and some preachers find it hard to distinguish the "American Way of Life" from the gospel. The regional mores of the South have sometimes muted the voice of the Southern Baptists. Given their membership concentration in one country and in one region of that country and their relatively short denominational history, the Southern Baptists strike some observers as more parochial and chauvinistic than Christians in the mainline Churches.

Worldwide, the largest group of Baptists outside of the U.S. are the 760,000 Baptists in India — followed by 539,000 in the Soviet Union, 442,000 in Brazil, 308,000 in Burma, 253,000 in the United Kingdom, and 246,000 in Zaire. The Baptist World Alliance reports only 250 Baptists in the Republic of Ireland, 161 in Greece, and 5,336 in Italy.

Southern Baptists belong to the Baptist World Alliance (founded in 1905) and support the Baptist Joint Committee on Public Affairs in Washington, D.C. They cooperate in the work of the American Bible Society, and in that of local ministerial and temperance organizations but shun membership in ecumenical agencies such as the World Council of Churches and the National Council of Churches.

American Baptists (Northern) belong to the National and World Councils of Churches. They also engage in dialogue with Roman Catholics. Few differences separate American Baptists and Disciples of Christ except that the latter observe Communion every Sunday. In some communities the two denominations have formed a single congregation embracing clergy and laity from both traditions. Liberal theologians, such as Harvey Cox, find a welcome in the American Baptist Churches but would probably have been evicted from a Southern Baptist seminary or college.

Current Trends

With some exceptions the Southern Baptists, like the South itself, can no longer be identified with charges of bigotry, anti-semitism, and anti-Catholicism which may have been true half a century ago. The assignment of Catholic employees to Southern plants and the move of Southern Baptists to northern cities have resulted in a new situation where far more Catholics and Baptists have become neighbors and friends.

Changes in Baptist Churches are evident in many areas. Newly ordained Baptist ministers can seldom be charged with modernism, but they show much greater awareness of what other Christians believe than their predecessors.

As One Baptist Sees It

Theologically, most Baptists affirm the central Christian beliefs shared by Catholics and Protestants of other traditions. A Southern Baptist leader in Baptist-Catholic dialogue writes:

In an age that threatens to deny any possibility of absolute truths it is good to know that there are many dogmas which Catholics and Baptists hold in common: God as a Person, Creator and Redeemer, Ruler and Judge of men, expressing himself in the Trinity; Jesus, Son of God, Savior through his atonement, and Lord of all through his resurrection; the Virgin Birth, miraculous ministry, present reign and final coming of Christ. We agree in general upon the inspiration of the Scriptures, the sinful state of man that demands God's saving grace, the primacy of love in Christian virtue, the sacredness of marriage and many others. In many of these truths we Baptists are closer to traditional Catholic teaching than we are to some liberal Protestant interpretations" (C. Brownlow Hastings, *A Baptist View of Changes in Roman Catholicism,* Home Mission Board, SBC, 1975).

From a Catholic Point of View

Since Roman Catholics and Baptists comprise the largest and second largest families of Christians in the U.S., it is inevitable that there will be an increasing number of Baptist-Catholic marriages. As we get to know each other in new jobs and in new neighborhoods, it is only a matter of time before fear of the unknown gives way to delight in the new.

As in any interfaith marriage, a number of religious and cultural differences are likely to surface. For example, most Baptists believe that total abstinence is the proper way of life for a Christian. A Catholic spouse who visits a Baptist church will find the surroundings much less familiar than would the partner in another interfaith marriage. The architecture and liturgy of a Lutheran or Episcopalian church would remind a Catholic of his home parish, but the Baptist churches stand solidly in the nonliturgical tradition. Simplicity is the watchword, and vestments, candles, a cross, stained glass, and formal prayers are exceptions.

The religious initiation and upbringing of children present problems in any interfaith marriage, but these problems may show up earlier in a Baptist-Catholic marriage. The Baptist spouse might object to the baptism of an infant in a Catholic church for reasons which would not bother a Methodist or Presbyterian. As we have seen, the Baptists regard baptism prior to a profession of faith as invalid.

Many Catholics would be uncomfortable with the fundamentalist approach to the Bible which is held by many Baptists and Baptist denominations. On the other hand, the liberalism of some members of the American (Northern) Baptist Churches would be equally uncongenial.

The major difficulty, however, in Baptist-Catholic marriages, lies, without a doubt, in the spouses' divergent views of the Eucharist. Under certain circumstances a Lutheran, Episcopalian, or Eastern Orthodox may receive Holy Communion in a Roman Catholic church. A Baptist, however, could hardly affirm that he or she shares the belief in the Real Presence which is required in such intercommunion. The Baptist considers the Lord's Supper a memorial whose meaning is mainly symbolic; most Christians believe it is a memorial — but much more than that.

6. Where Do You Go from Here?

Today, more than ever in the past, Catholic Christians would seem to be open to what their new Baptist co-workers and friends have in such abundance: evangelistic enthusiasm, a deep sense of local church community, and an openness to the poor and the unsophisticated. The U.S. Catholic bishops have called evangelization the essential task of the Church; they have stressed parish renewal as the ultimate thrust of Vatican II; and they have called for identification with the poor. It seems that needs we have recognized are, perhaps, being providentially taken care of.

It can only be hoped that more and more rank-and-file Christians of both traditions will put aside old animosities and learn from each others' distinct faith-formed outlooks. In increasing numbers then, couples will also bring these complementary visions into lives of Christian intimacy in the marital state.

Such couples may indeed fear that they are in danger of estranging themselves from the separate communities through which the gift of faith came to them and through which it should be nourished. This sensitivity is indeed praiseworthy. But just what should couples do?

Contrary to the opinion of some, it is best that both members in such an interfaith union become more deeply involved with heart and mind in their respective Churches and more conversant with the wealth of their divergent traditions.

Such a practice need anticipate no compromise, no demeaning or conscience-disturbing admission, in practice or otherwise, that the doctrine of either Church is lacking in fullness. It will rather give expression to a simple and humble admission that the development of faith in the Christians engaged in dialogue is in progress, and a consequent eagerness on the part of both to share with each other the growth in faith that each gratefully accepts as gift.

In this sharing, interfaith couples should find reassurance in the words of Bishop J. Francis Stafford to the world synod of Catholic Bishops in 1980, in which he referred to interfaith marriages as "a special opportunity for Christian growth." He insists that such couples not be led "to ignore the real differences which exist in their faith orientation" but be encouraged to "search out and amplify areas of communality, truths on which they discover agreement and expressions of piety which bring both to a deeper awareness of God." The spokesman for the American bishops goes on to say: "What is behind this strategy is a belief in the authenticity of both faith orientations, if held in good conscience, and a hope that from their combination in the conjugal love, there will result a deeper marital union."

It goes without saying, of course, that if the non-Catholic partner feels called in his or her faith growth to join the Catholic Church, the Catholic partner will in no manner discourage him or her in this. This also is the intent of the Council fathers' respectful statement on *Religious Liberty* (3). "He is bound to follow this conscience faithfully in all his activity so that he may come to God, who is his last end. Therefore he must not be forced to act contrary to his conscience. Nor must he be prevented from acting according to his conscience, especially in religious matters."

We hope and pray that this booklet will help interfaith couples share the vision of faith. The absence of any kind of "discussion starters" is not an oversight; we felt that it would be presumptive, in matters so personal, to formulate the gifts that intimacy urges you to share.

Further Reading

Armstrong, O. K. and Armstrong, Majorie Moore. *The Indomitable Baptists.* Garden City, New York, Doubleday, 1967.

Baker, Robert A. *The Southern Baptist Convention and Its People 1607-1972.* Nashville, Broadman, 1974.

Encyclopedia of Southern Baptists. 2 vols. Nashville, Broadman, 1972.

Hastings, C. Brownlow. *Introducing Southern Baptists.* New York, Paulist Press, 1981.

Lawless, Richard M. *When Love Unites the Church.* St. Meinrad, Indiana, Abbey Press, 1982.

Odle, Joe T. *Why I Am a Baptist.* Nashville, Broadman, 1972.

Torbet, Robert G. *A History of the Baptists.* rev. ed., Valley Forge, Pa., Judson Press, 1963.

REACHING OUT WITH HEART AND MIND

A series of booklets that explore the history, beliefs, and traditions of the larger Christian Churches in the United States. $1.50 each.

Other booklets in this series from Liguori Publications include:

Reaching Out to THE METHODISTS with Heart and Mind

Reaching Out to THE LUTHERANS with Heart and Mind

Reaching Out to THE PRESBYTERIANS and THE REFORMED with Heart and Mind

Reaching Out to THE EPISCOPALIANS with Heart and Mind

Order from your local bookstore or write to:
Liguori Publications, Box 060, Liguori, Missouri 63057
(Please add 50¢ postage and handling for the first item
ordered and 25¢ for each additional item.)